STOCKING STUMPERS®

GOLF EDITION

By **S. Claus**
with help from **John Murphy**

Red-Letter Press, Inc.

STOCKING STUMPERS- Golf Edition
Copyright ©1997 Red-Letter Press, Inc.
ISBN: 0-940462-57-5
Printed in the United States of America

For information address Red-Letter Press, Inc.
P.O. Box 393, Saddle River, NJ 07458

ACKNOWLEDGMENTS

A Stocking Stumpers salute to Santa's "subordinate clauses":

Cover design and typography: **s.w.artz, inc.**

Illustrations: **Jack Kreismer, Sr.**

Editorial: **Ellen Fischbein and Geoff Scowcroft**

Contributors: **Angela Demers, Russ Edwards and Jack Kreismer**

A Personal Message from Santa

'Twas the Night Before Christmas
and I left the North Pole
to bring to your stocking
a fresh lump of coal;
But St. Nick's got heart
and your sins weren't voluminous,
so I brought you a gift
in lieu of bituminous;
Now since you've escaped
my long list of lumpers,
I've left you instead
Santa's favorite, Stocking Stumpers.
Merry Christmas!

S. Claus

FIRST NAMES FIRST

Santa's making his list (and checking it twice). Help him out by giving him the real first names of each of the following golfers.

1. Chip Beck
2. Chi Chi Rodriguez
3. J.C. Snead
4. Tiger Woods
5. Fuzzy Zoeller

ANSWERS

1. Charles Beck
2. Juan Rodriguez
3. Jesse Carlyle Snead
4. Eldrick Woods
5. Frank Zoeller - his middle name
   is Urban, which explains his nickname.

DEAR JOHNS

The answer to each of the following questions is someone named John.

6. This John is the only man to win the U.S. Open and the U.S. Junior Amateur.

7. Who said, "I hate this bump-and-run junk," when referring to the British Open and then won it at St. Andrews three years later?

8. This golfer finished second at the 1992 British Open (he led until the 72nd hole) and shot a 26-under-par score at the 1996 Memphis Open.

9. Who was the first American to win the U.S. Open and also the youngest winner of a PGA Tour event?

10. He defeated Tom Watson and Jerry Pate in a play-off to win the 1978 PGA Championship. Who is he?

ANSWERS

6. Johnny Miller
7. John Daly
8. John Cook
9. John McDermott
10. John Mahaffey

HOME SWEET HOME

Name the native country of each of the following golfers.

11. Steve Elkington
12. Ernie Els
13. Bernhard Langer
14. Nick Price
15. Ian Woosnam

ANSWERS

11. Elkington - Australia

12. Els - South Africa

13. Langer - Germany

14. Price - South Africa (Note: Although Price was born in South Africa and lives in Florida, he's a Zimbabwean with a British passport. He also served two years in the Rhodesian Air Force.)

15. Woosnam - Wales

TRUE OR FALSE

16. It is legal to use a pool cue as a putter.
17. Golf was once an Olympic sport.
18. Richard Burton competed in and won the British Open.
19. A native Japanese player won a U.S. Tour event.
20. Kim Jong Il, president of North Korea, got 5 holes-in-one in one round at the Pyongyang Golf Club.

ANSWERS

16. False - it was banned in an 1895 ruling.

17. True - it was played in 1900 and 1904.

18. True - he won in 1939. Of course, it wasn't the Richard Burton who married Liz Taylor.

19. True - Isao Aoki won the 1983 Hawaiian Open.

20. If you believe the pro at the Pyongyang Golf Club, it's true. Of course, he also claimed that Kim shot a 38-under-par 34 for the day.

THE GOLDEN BEAR

21. What is Jack Nicklaus' real first name?
22. In what state was he born?
23. What college did he attend?
24. How many professional Majors has he won?
25. What is the only Major which he hasn't won?
26. What is the name of the course which he designed and at which the Memorial Tournament is held each year?

ANSWERS

21. Jack
22. (Columbus) Ohio
23. Ohio State
24. 18 - six Masters, five PGA Championships,
    four U.S. Opens and three British Opens
25. The British Amateur - he won two U.S. Amateurs.
26. Muirfield Village Golf Club

COMMON LINKS

Find the common link in each list below.

27. Prestwick in 1860, Newport in 1895, Siwanoy in 1916
    and Augusta in 1934

28. Oakmont in 1962, Baltusrol in 1967, Pebble Beach in
    1972 and Baltusrol in 1980

29. St. Andrews, The Country Club, Shinnecock Hills,
    Newport and Chicago - all in 1894

30. Carnoustie in 1975, Turnberry in 1977, Muirfield in
    1980, Royal Troon in 1982 and Royal Birkdale in 1983

31. Inwood in 1923, Scioto in 1926, Winged Foot in 1929
    and Interlachen in 1930

ANSWERS

27. The first course at which each of the professional
    Majors was played

28. The courses at which Jack Nicklaus won his U.S. Opens

29. The five charter members of the USGA,
    which was founded in 1894

30. The courses at which Tom Watson won
    his British Opens

31. The courses at which Bobby Jones won his U.S. Opens

THE ALMIGHTY DOLLAR

32. Who was the first player to pass a million dollars in career earnings on the Tour?

33. Who was the first to win a million dollars in one year on the Tour?

34. In 1994, Fuzzy Zoeller won more than a million dollars on the Tour. What was remarkable about that?

35. In 1996, a player passed 10 million dollars in career earnings. Who?

36. What is the richest tournament in the world?

ANSWERS

32. Arnold Palmer
33. Curtis Strange, in 1988
34. He didn't win a tournament that year.
35. Greg Norman
36. The Players Tournament Championship

WHERE IN THE WORLD

*As a world traveler, Santa knows where all the famous courses are located.
Do you? Name the country for each list.*

37. Chantilly, Golf de St-Nom-la-Breteche Le Tocquet, Morfontaine and Seignosse
38. Ballybunion, Lahinch, Portmarnock and County Louth
39. Carnoustie, Gleneagles, Prestwick and Turnberry
40. Club de Campo, El Saler, Sotogrande and Valderrama
41. Castle Harbour, Mid-Ocean, Port Royal and St. George's
42. Commonwealth, Kingston Heath, Royal Adelaide and Victoria

ANSWERS

37. France
38. Ireland
39. Scotland
40. Spain
41. Bermuda
42. Australia

POTPOURRI

43. Name one of the three golfers who have U.S. Stamps honoring them.

44. In 1978, Bob Impaglia made history by becoming the first player penalized at the U.S. Open for a certain infraction. What was it?

45. At the Players Championship in 1992, John Daly and Mark Calcavecchia were fined by the PGA Tour. What did they do?

46. In 1938, Roy Ainsley was two strokes behind the leader going into the 16th hole of the last round of the U.S. Open. Within five, what did he score on the 16th?

47. What's the record for throwing a ball around a course?

ANSWERS

43. Bobby Jones, Babe Didrickson Zaharias, and Francis Ouimet

44. He was penalized for slow play.

45. They played too quickly. When they finished in 2 hours and 5 minutes, they were fined for not trying to do their best.

46. He got a 19. 13 of these strokes were taken trying to get his ball out of a creek.

47. 82

LPGA

48. Name the current four professional Women's Majors.

49. Which of these four is always played on the same course?

50. Which one is played outside the United States?

51. Who is the only woman to win all four of these Majors?

52. Name one of the two Swedes who have won the U.S. Women's Open.

53. At the 1992 LPGA Championship, this woman became the first to shoot four sub-70 rounds in a Major. Name her.

ANSWERS

48. Dinah Shore, U.S. Women's Open, du
    Maurier Classic and LPGA Championship

49. The Dinah Shore - it's always played at the
    Mission Hills Country Club
    in Rancho Mirage, CA.

50. The du Maurier - it's played in Canada.

51. Pat Bradley

52. Liselotte Neumann and Annika Sorenstam

53. Betsy King - she shot 68-66-67-66.

THE WORLD ACCORDING TO CHI CHI

The vowels have been deleted from some famous Chi Chi Rodriguez lines.
See if you can decode them.

54. FR MST MTRS, TH BST WD N THR BG S TH PNCL.

55. 'M PLNG LK TRZN - ND SCRNG LK JN.

56. T'S STLL MBRRSSNG. SKD M CDD FR SND WDG, ND TN
MNTS LTR H CM BCK WTH HM N R.

ANSWERS

54. "For most amateurs, the best wood in their bag is the pencil."

55. "I'm playing like Tarzan - and scoring like Jane."

56. "It's still embarrassing. I asked my caddy for a sand wedge, and ten minutes later he came back with a ham on rye."

CUPS

Help yourself to a cup of eggnog if you can name these famous Cups from the descriptions below.

57. Male amateurs of Great Britain and Ireland versus the male amateurs of the United States.

58. Female amateurs of Great Britain and Ireland versus the female amateurs of the United States.

59. Male European pros versus male pros of the United States.

60. Female European pros versus the female pros of the United States.

61. Male pros of the Unites States versus male pros from other non-European countries.

62. For a bonus cup of Christmas cheer: List the above five competitions in age order.

ANSWERS

57. Walker Cup

58. Curtis Cup

59. Ryder Cup

60. Solheim Cup

61. Presidents Cup

62. The first year of competition for each Cup was: Walker - 1922, Ryder - 1927, Curtis - 1932, Solheim - 1990 and Presidents - 1994.

ALL IN THE FAMILY

63. At the 1964 Masters, he led after the first round. The day after the tournament ended, his son was born. In 1995, that son finished second at the Masters. Name father and son.

64. Two pairs of fathers and sons have won the British Open. You should get one pair.

65. Brothers Dave and Danny combined to win the 1980 Disney World Team Championship. What's their family name?

66. Name the brothers who have each won over 2.5 million dollars on the PGA Tour. The older brother won the 1977 PGA Championship while the younger brother never won a tournament.

67. Name the runner-up at the 1973 Masters whose uncle was a three-time winner of the tournament.

ANSWERS

63. Davis Love, II and III

64. Old and Young Tom Morris and Willie Park, Sr. and Jr.

65. Edwards

66. Lanny and Bobby Wadkins - older bother Lanny also won the 1970 U.S. Amateur.

67. J.C. Snead - his uncle was, of course, the famous Sam Snead.

GIVE ME A VOWEL

Below is a list of five players' first and last names without vowels. (The order of the consonants has not been changed.) How many of these can you get?

Hint: Each has won a Major.

68. LTRVN
69. JRRPT
70. HLRWN
71. NWSNM
72. RNLS

ANSWERS

68. Lee Trevino
69. Jerry Pate
70. Hale Irwin
71. Ian Woosnam
72. Ernie Els

CADDY SHACK

73. In 1986, who was Jack Nicklaus' caddy when he won his sixth Masters?

74. What's the nickname of Jeff Medlin, who caddied for John Daly and Nick Price when they won their PGA Championships?

75. True or False: Caddies over the age of 16 are considered professional golfers.

76. Fanny Sunesson has caddied for what golfer when he won his Majors?

77. In the 1946 U.S. Open, Byron Nelson's caddy accidentally kicked Nelson's ball. What was the call?

ANSWERS

73. Jack Nicklaus, Jr.

74. Squeeky

75. Today, this is false. But in 1909 the USGA ruled that a caddy over the age of 16 was a professional golfer. The rule was amended in 1963.

76. Nick Faldo

77. Nelson got a one-stroke penalty. As a result, he finished regulation tied with Lloyd Mangrum. He lost the play-off the next day.

AMATEUR HOUR

78. The answer is not Bobby Jones; it's Johnny Goodman. What's the question?

79. Who competed in the British Amateur, won an Oscar for Best Actor and had a son who won the U.S. Amateur?

80. *Golf Digest* ranked what player as the number one amateur of the year from 1959 through 1961?

81. Name one of the four amateurs to win PGA Tour Events since 1950.

82. Only two golfers have won the Sullivan Award which is given to the Outstanding Amateur Athlete of the Year. Name one of them.

83. Name all the amateurs who have won the Masters.

ANSWERS

78. Who was the last amateur to win the U.S. Open? He did this in 1933.

79. Bing Crosby - his son, Nathaniel, won the 1981 U.S. Amateur.

80. Jack Nicklaus

81. Gene Littler, in 1954; Doug Sanders, in 1956; Scott Verplank, in 1985; and Phil Mickelson, in 1991

82. Bobby Jones, in 1930 and Lawson Little, in 1935

83. No amateur has ever won the Masters.

PHRASE CRAZE

Decode the following golf terms.

84.

85. a putt

86.
    $$\frac{2}{\text{par}}$$

ANSWERS

84. A hole-in-one
85. A short putt
86. 2-over-par

U.S. OPEN

Match the accomplishment at the U.S. Open with the player on the right.

87. Shot a 63 in the final round.
88. Won U.S. Amateur and Open in same year.
89. At one point was 12-under-par.
90. Only man to win exactly three times
91. 2/3 of his career wins.
92. Shot 282 as an amateur.

A - Hale Irwin
B - Bobby Jones
C - Johnny Miller
D - Gil Morgan
E - Jack Nicklaus
F - Andy North

ANSWERS

87. C - Johnny Miller - he did this at the 1973 Open at Oakmont.

88. B - Bobby Jones, in 1930 - Chick Evans, Jr. also did this, in 1916.

89. D - Dr. Gil Morgan - he accomplished this at Pebble Beach in 1992.
    No other golfer has ever reached -10. He collapsed in the last two rounds
    and wound up five-over-par for the tournament.

90. A - Hale Irwin

91. F- Andy North

92. E - Jack Nicklaus - no amateur has ever shot better.

TOM-TOMS

Which Toms could have made the following statements?

93. I never won the Masters but finished second four times (1969, '72, '74, '75). In 1980 I got a 13 on the par-3 twelfth hole at Augusta.

94. I won three of the first five British Opens and finished second the other two times.

95. A college teammate of Ben Crenshaw, I won the U.S. Open at Pebble Beach in '92.

96. I was the first player to five-putt at the Masters (in '96). Fortunately, when I was younger, I won the Masters twice.

97. Alphabetically, I'm the first player to win a Major.

ANSWERS

93. Tom Weiskopf
94. Old Tom Morris
95. Tom Kite
96. Tom Watson
97. Tommy Aaron

MAJORS

98. Who is the only man to win three professional Majors in the same year? Hint: He did it in 1953.

99. 1994 was an unusual year for Americans. Why?

100. In 1986, the same player led all four professional Majors after 54 holes. He won only one of them. Who?

101. What's the only professional Major in which a tie after regulation is still decided by a minimum of 18 extra holes?

102. What's the only professional Major at which no player has shot four rounds in the 60s?

ANSWERS

98. Ben Hogan

99. For the first time, no American won any of the four professional Majors.

100. Greg Norman

101. The U.S. Open

102. The Masters

QUOTE - UNQUOTE

Name the golfers being referred to.

103. "He hits his divots farther than I hit my drives."
104. "I don't know; I've never played there."
105. "His face is that of a warthog after it bit a wasp."
106. "He plays a game with which I am not familiar."
107. "The only way I'll ever make a Ryder Cup
     team is when I'm captain; then I can name
     myself to the team."

ANSWERS

103. John Daly, by David Feherty

104. Tiger Woods, by Sandy Lyle - obviously, Lyle thought Tiger Woods was a course.

105. Colin Montgomerie, by David Feherty

106. Jack Nicklaus, by Bobby Jones

107. John Daly, about himself

COMMON LINKS

Find the common link for each question below.

Hint: Each has something to do with Majors.

108. Gene Sarazen, Ben Hogan, Jack Nicklaus and Gary Player
109. Willie Park, Horace Rawlins, Jim Barnes and Horton Smith
110. Old Tom Morris, Hale Irwin, Julius Boros and Jack Nicklaus
111. Walter Hagen, John McDermott, Walter Hagen and Horton Smith
112. Young Tom Morris, John McDermott, Gene Sarazen and Tiger Woods

ANSWERS

108. The only four men to win all four professional Majors
109. The first winners of the four professionals Majors
110. The oldest winner of each of the four professionals Majors
111. The first native-born American to win each of the four professional Majors
112. The youngest winner of each of the four professional Majors

Note: In the last four answers, the winners are given in the order of British Open, U.S. Open, PGA Championship and Masters.

SCRAMBLE

Santa's computer has jumbled his list! Help him out by unscrambling the last names of the golfers listed below. Hint: All have won professional Majors.

113. TAN SOW
114. MR LEAP
115. VEIN ROT
116. AS IN LUCK
117. NEW CRASH

ANSWERS

113. (Tom) Watson
114. (Arnold) Palmer
115. (Lee) Trevino
116. (Jack) Nicklaus
117. (Ben) Crenshaw

U.S. OPEN

118. Who is the only winner to have played exactly 91 holes in the Open?

119. Name the only lefty to finish a U.S. Open at par or better.

120. What amateur finished second at the 1960 Open?

121. Who is the only man to win wearing glasses and win again when he wasn't wearing glasses?

122. Who shot a 75 in the play-off in 1991 and still won?

ANSWERS

118. Hale Irwin - he beat Mike Donald in 91 holes at the 1990 Open.
119. Phil Mickelson
120. Jack Nicklaus
121. Hale Irwin - the last time he won, he was wearing contacts.
122. Payne Stewart - he beat Scott Simpson, who shot a 77 at Hazeltine National that day.

OF COURSE, OF COURSE

Name the golf courses described below.

123. Permanent host of the Tournament Players Championship, it's known for its island green at the 17th hole

124. Course at which the Masters is played

125. The South Carolina course which was awarded the 1991 Ryder Cup even before the course was completed

126. The course whose 17th hole is called the Road Hole

127. The public course at which Tom Watson won a U.S. Open in 1982

ANSWERS

123. The Tournament Players Club at Sawgrass
124. Augusta National
125. The Ocean Course at Kiawah Island
126. Old Course at St. Andrews
127. Pebble Beach

REAL WINNERS

128. Five PGA players have been fortunate enough to win three straight tournaments since 1960. Name one of them.

129. The PGA record for winning consecutive tournaments is 11. What Texan holds this record?

130. Two players won at least one tournament for 17 consecutive years. Name one of them.

131. In 1972 and 1973, what golfing legend won seven tournaments each year?

132. Who has won the most PGA Tour Events?

ANSWERS

128. Billy Casper - 1960; Arnold Palmer - '60 and '62; Johnny Miller - '74; Hubert Green - '76; and Gary Player - '78

129. Byron Nelson, in 1945

130. Arnold Palmer, 1955 - '71 and Jack Nicklaus, 1962 - '78

131. Jack Nicklaus

132. Sam Snead

WHAT'S IN A NAME?

133. What winner of a Major is named after Jesus' parents?

134. Three players with the letter z in their last names have defeated Greg Norman in play-offs to win Majors. Name them.

135. What player who has won a Major has a month for a last name?

136. Ted Ray won Majors in the early part of this century. Name another player with exactly three letters in his last name who has won a Major.

137. Since World War II, there have been four players who have won professional Majors whose first and family names begin with the same letter. Sam Snead is obviously one of them. Name one of the other three.

ANSWERS

133. Jose-Maria Olazabal
134. Fuzzy Zoeller, Larry Mize and Paul Azinger
135. Don January
136. Ernie Els
137. Scott Simpson, Ernie Els and Charles Coody

IN OTHER WORDS

Golfers speak their own language - especially when it comes to scoring. Can you help Santa and Rudolph shed some light on the following expressions?

138. I got a snowman on that hole.

139. Give me a Laurel and Hardy.

140. I'm dormie.

141. I got an albatross.

142. I'm going to take a mulligan.

ANSWERS

138. I got an 8.
139. Give me a 10 on that hole.
140. Used in match play, it indicates that I'm as many holes up as there are holes remaining to be played.
141. A double-eagle
142. A do-over - my original shot won't count. In regulation play, mulligans are not allowed. (Originally, mulligans were only taken on the initial shot of the day. Some players, however, allow themselves numerous mulligans during a round.)

AFRICAN-AMERICANS

143. True or False: As recently as 1961, the PGA constitution stated that only whites could play on the PGA Tour.

144. The first African-American to win a PGA Tour Event did so in 1967 when he won the Greater Hartford Open. Name him.

145. Who was the first African-American to play in the Masters?

146. Who won the Vardon Trophy for having the best average on the Tour in 1984?

147. Who is the only three-time winner of the U.S. Junior Amateur and the youngest winner of the U.S. Amateur?

ANSWERS

143. True - until November, 1961, the PGA constitution stated that only Caucasians could be members of the Association and play on the Tour.

144. Charles Sifford

145. Lee Elder, in 1975

146. Calvin Peete

147. Tiger Woods

ARNIE

148. In what state was Arnold Palmer born?

149. What college did he attend?

150. What's the name of the group of fans which follows him on the course?

151. The Arnold Palmer Award each year is given to whom?

152. Which professional Major did he not win?

153. What was the first Major that he won?

ANSWERS

148. (Latrobe) Pennsylvania
149. Wake Forest
150. Arnie's Army
151. The leading money winner on the Tour
152. The PGA Championship
153. The 1954 U.S. Amateur

WAY BACK WHEN

154. Name the 14-year-old who won the Georgia State Amateur Championship. He qualified that year for the U.S. Amateur Championship and went to the third round before he lost in match play.

155. In 1973, the Golf Writers Association of America selected its five greatest golfers of all time. How many can you get?

156. Three players won more than ten tournaments in a year. If I tell you that all were born in 1912, you should be able to get all three.

157. Only one golfer has ever won six British Opens. Hint: This "father of modern golf" has a grip named after him.

158. The last regular PGA Tour Event which Arnold Palmer won was in 1973. He played 90 holes. Name the Event.

ANSWERS

154. Bobby Jones
155. Walter Hagen, Ben Hogan, Bobby Jones, Jack Nicklaus and Arnold Palmer.
156. Ben Hogan, Sam Snead and Byron Nelson
157. Harry Vardon
158. The Bob Hope Classic

MASTERS

159. Name the two Spanish golfers who have won the Masters.

160. When Tom Watson missed the cut in 1996 it stopped a streak of 21 consecutive years. Who holds the record at 24?

161. Who is the only player to win two Masters play-offs?

162. Name one of the two players to win consecutive Masters.

163. The best round shot by a left-hander at the Masters is 65. Who did it?

ANSWERS

159. Seve Ballesteros and Jose-Maria Olazabal
160. Sam Snead
161. Nick Faldo
162. Jack Nicklaus and Nick Faldo
163. Phil Mickelson

NICK-NAMES

The answer to each of these questions is a St. Nick sound-alike.

164. The record for the lowest 18-hole score at the Masters is 63. What African player did this in 1986?

165. What Brit won two British Opens during the 1990s?

166. Who shot the lowest score at a PGA Championship - 271? Hint: This was his only Major win.

167. Until Tiger Woods broke the record in 1997, 271 was also the best score ever shot at the Masters, a mark shared by two golfers. One is Raymond Floyd. Who's the other?

ANSWERS

164. Nick Price
165. Nick Faldo
166. Bobby Nichols
167. Jack Nicklaus

LINKS LINGO

What is the background of each of the following golf terms?

168. Tee
169. Caddie
170. Bogey
171. Birdie

ANSWERS

168. Tee comes from the Scottish word teay, which means a pile of sand. (Before the invention of the wooden tee, sand was used to raise the ball.)

169. Caddie probably comes from the French word cadet, which is pronounced cadday. Young attendants in royal courts were called cadets.

170. At the Royal Yarmouth Golf Club, members created an imaginary member Colonel Bogey (similar to the bogey man) who always shot par. With the improvement in equipment, his score became one over par.

171. The word birdie has been traced to 1898 when it was a shortened form of "a bird of a hole."

MAJORS

172. Since 1960, only three rookies have won Majors. Name one of them.

173. What player was leading a professional Major by six strokes going into the last round and lost?

174. There have been six players who have won at least eight professional Majors. Name half of them.

175. What player within the past twenty years lost play-offs in all four professional Majors?

176. What European has won the most Majors in the past fifty years?

ANSWERS

172. Jack Nicklaus, Jerry Pate and John Daly.

173. This happened to Greg Norman at the '96 Masters.

174. Jack Nicklaus - 18; Walter Hagen - 11; Ben Hogan and Gary Player - 9; and Tom Watson and Arnold Palmer - 8

175. Greg Norman

176. Nick Faldo

ELEMENTARY, MY DEAR WATSON

177. In what state was Tom Watson born?

178. What college did he attend?

179. Which professional Major did he not win?

180. How many professional Majors did he win?

ANSWERS

177. (Kansas City) Missouri
178. Stanford
179. The PGA Championship
180. 8 - five British Opens, Two
     Masters and a U.S. Open

RYDER CUP

181. Only two men played in ten or more consecutive Ryder Cup competitions. Name one of them.

182. In '91, the 1989 British Open champ was dormie 4 over Colin Montgomerie and didn't win. He finished up triple bogey, bogey, triple bogey, bogey to let Montgomerie escape with half a point. Name this player.

183. Talking about '91, name the European player whose missed putt on the last hole of the tournament enabled the American team to escape with a tie.

184. Who is the oldest participant in Ryder Cup competition? He was 51 when he played for the Americans in 1993.

185. On what Jack Nicklaus-designed course did the Americans lose on home turf for the first time (in 1987)?

ANSWERS

181. Nick Faldo and Christy O'Conner, Jr.
182. Mark Calcavecchia
183. Bernhard Langer
184. Ray Floyd
185. Muirfield Village

HOW LOW CAN YOU GO?

186. Who holds the PGA Tour record for lowest score over 72 holes?

187. Who was the first player to shoot a score lower than his age in a PGA tournament?

188. What is the lowest round at a PGA Tour Event and what two men shot it?

189. In the third round of the 1980 U.S. Open at Baltusrol, Hubert Green did something remarkable from the 9th hole to the 16th. What was it?

190. The record for nine holes at a U.S. Open is 29. What man accomplished this twice?

ANSWERS

186. Mike Souchak — he shot 60-68-64-65 for a 27-under-par 257.

187. Sam Snead - he shot a 66 in 1979 at the Quad Cities Open when he was 67.

188. 59 - Chip Beck and Al Geiberger did it.

189. He scored a three on each hole. He got three pars and five birdies.

190. Neal Lancaster, at Shinnecock Hills (in 1995) and at Oakland Hills the following year

FAVORITE SONS

*Each of the following winners of a Major has a last name ending in SON.
How many can you get?*

191. He won the U.S. Open in 1983 and the PGA Championship in 1981 and '87.

192. He won five British Opens.

193. The only Ladies' professional Major this Australian didn't win was the Dinah Shore.

194. The only professional Major he didn't win was the British Open.

195. This Australian won four British Opens (in 1955, '56, '58 and '65).

ANSWERS

191. Larry Nelson
192. Tom Watson
193. Jan Stephenson
194. Byron Nelson
195. Peter Thomson

WHO'S WHO

*The following clues suggest the last names of six players who won the U.S. Open.
Each name has exactly one syllable. Can you come up with the
"who" for each "what"?*

196. A color
197. A direction
198. Something that you fly
199. Unusual
200. The top of the head
201. A spot of color

ANSWERS

196. (Hubert) Green
197. (Andy) North
198. (Tom) Kite
199. (Curtis) Strange
200. (Jerry) Pate
201. (Jack) Fleck

SCRAMBLED II

Santa's new software has struck again! Help him figure out the five Masters winners whose last names are scrambled below.

202. LOSE CUP
203. GEL RAN
204. DO FLY
205. TEES OR BALLS
206. FED DOC FILM

ANSWERS

202. (Fred) Couples
203. (Bernhard) Langer
204. (Raymond) Floyd
205. (Seve) Ballesteros
206. (Dr. Cary) Middlecoff

COMMON LINKS

Find the common link for each of the following groups.

207. Jerry Pate, Nick Price, Doug Weaver, and Mark Wiebe
208. Phil Mickelson, Bob Charles, Russ Cochran and Blaine McCallister
209. Jock Hutchison, Jim Barnes, Cyril Walker and Tommy Armour
210. Tom Wargo, Larry Mowry, Simon Hobday, Larry Laoretti and Jim Albus

ANSWERS

207. All four got a hole-in-one on the par-3 sixth hole in the same round of the 1989 U.S. Open held at Oak Hill. Previously, only 17 holes-in-one had been gotten in the history of the Open.

208. All four of these men putt left-handed. Note: They do not all play left-handed since McCallister, except for putting, plays right-handed.

209. All are native-born Brits who had become naturalized Americans by the time they won their Majors in the 1920s and '30s.

210. All won Senior Majors within the past twenty years without ever winning on the regular PGA Tour.

WOMEN

Here are a few of Mrs. Claus' favorites.

211. Six women have won back-to-back U.S. Opens. How many can you get?
212. Which one of these women holds the record for the U.S. Women's Open best score?
213. In 1995, what woman missed the U.S. Open cut for the first time in 26 appearances?
214. What Olympic gold medal winner won the 1948, '50 and '54 U.S. Women's Opens?
215. What British woman is the first to win a million dollars in a year?

ANSWERS

211. Mickey Wright, in 1958 and '59; Donna Caponi, in 1969 and '70;
     Susie Berning, in 1972 and '73; Hollis Stacy, in 1977 and '78;
     Betsy King, in 1989 and '90; and Annika Sorenstam, in 1995 and '96

212. Annika Sorenstam - she shot an 8-under-par 272 at Southern Pines,
     NC, in 1996.

213. JoAnne (Big Momma) Carner

214. Babe Didrickson Zaharias

215. Laura Davies, in 1994 - she played on five different tours that year.

DIS-COURSE

*Each of the following is a quote about a course - minus the vowels.
See if you can decode them.*

216. TH NL PLC THT'S HLR THN ST. NDRWS S WSTMNSTR BB.

217. TH CLST THNG T HVN FR GLFR , ND JST BT S DFFCLT T
     GT NT.

218. GD SWMP, SPLD.

ANSWERS

216. "The only place that's holier than St. Andrews is Westminster Abbey."
Sam Snead

217. "The closest thing to heaven for a golfer, and just about as difficult to get into."
Joe Gershwiler, talking about Augusta National

218. "A good swamp, spoiled."
Gary Player, talking about the Carnoustie Golf Club

Note: Player was, of course, mirroring Mark Twain's definition of the sport: "Golf, a good walk spoiled."

BEN AND SAMMY

219. What is Hogan's real first name?

220. True or False: Hogan was born in Dublin.

221. Hogan won the British Open in 1953 to complete a career Grand Slam. How many times did he compete in this tournament?

222. In what state was Sam Snead born?

223. What was Snead's nickname?

224. What's the only professional Major which Sam didn't win?

ANSWERS

219. William.

220. True - of course, it was Dublin, Texas.

221. Only that once

222. (Hot Springs) Virginia

223. Slammin' Sammy

224. The U.S. Open - he was the runner-up four times.

THE BRITISH OPEN

225. Golfers from ten countries have won the British Open. Name seven.

226. No Italian has ever won but one got close. What Italian lost a play-off for the title?

227. Since World War II, there have been three Americans who have successfully defended their British Open titles. Name them.

228. In the last twenty years, there have been two golfers with more than ten letters in their last names who have won. Name them both.

229. In 1993, this golfer was the first champion to shoot four rounds in the 60s. His closing round 64 was the finest closing round by any winner in the history of the British Open. Who accomplished this?

ANSWERS

225. Scotland, United States, England, Australia, South Africa, Spain, France, Ireland, New Zealand and Argentina

226. Costantino Rocca

227. Arnold Palmer - 1962; Lee Trevino - in '72; and Tom Watson - in '83

228. Seve Ballesteros and Mark Calcavecchia

229. Greg Norman

THE WINNER'S CIRCLE

230. Who was the first winner of the Byron Nelson Tournament (in 1944)?

231. When Fred Couples won the Masters in 1992, he was the first player since Ben Hogan to win not using a certain piece of golf equipment. What was it?

232. Walter Hagen won his second PGA Championship in Larry Bird's hometown. What was the name of the course?

233. Tom Kite (in 1992) and Orville Moody (in 1969) are the only two golfers to win the U.S. Open doing what on the green?

234. In 1960 and in 1972, golfers, in attempting to win the Grand Slam, won the Masters and the U.S. Open, but finished second in the British Open. Name these two golfers.

ANSWERS

230. Byron Nelson
231. A golf glove
232. French Lick Golf Club
233. Putting cross-handed
234. Arnold Palmer and Jack Nicklaus

THE LONG AND SHORT OF IT

235. What course has the shortest hole on the PGA Tour?

236. Within 20 yards, what's the longest hole on the PGA Tour?

237. Who, at 5' 4", is the smallest winner of the Masters?

238. In 1936, a club-throwing tournament was held in Atlanta. Within ten yards, what was the longest throw?

ANSWERS

235. Pebble Beach - it's seventh hole is 107 yards.

236. The 644-yard first hole at Castle Pines Golf Club in Castle Rock, Colorado - it's a par-5.

237. Ian Woosnam

238. 61 yards

SUPER MEX

239. In what state was Lee Trevino born?

240. What college did he attend?

241. What unusual thing happened to him at the Western Open in 1975?

242. Which professional Major did he not win?

243. In 1971, in three consecutive weeks, he won three countries' Open Championships. Name these countries.

ANSWERS

239. (Dallas) Texas

240. Trevino did not attend college.

241. He got hit by lightning.

242. He never won the Masters. He always said that Augusta National was not suited to his game. He won two U.S. Opens, two PGA Championships and two British Opens.

243. United States, Canada and Great Britain.

MAPPING IT OUT

Each of the courses listed on the left has hosted at least two U.S. Opens. Match the courses with the locations on the right.

244. Baltusrol
245. Canterbury
246. The Country Club
247. Hazeltine National
248. The Olympic Club
249. Shinnecock Hills
250. Winged Foot

A - Brookline, MA
B - Chaska, MN
C - Cleveland, OH
D - Mamaroneck, NY
E - San Francisco, CA
F - Southhampton, NY
G - Springfield, NJ

ANSWERS

244. Baltusrol - G - Springfield, NJ
245. Canterbury - C - Cleveland, OH
246. The Country Club - A - Brookline, MA
247. Hazeltine National - B - Chaska, MN
248. The Olympic Club - E - San Francisco, CA
249. Shinnecock Hills - F - Southampton, NY
250. Winged Foot - D - Mamaroneck, NY